# Political Partisanship, Cyberbullying, & Suicidal Thoughts

Authors:

Yuan Peng, MSCJ

Wayne L. Davis, Ph.D.

Illustrator:

Dawn Larder

LoGiudice Publishing
Orland, IN 46776


Library of Congress Control Number: 2021904912

# Abstract

There is a difference between Democrats and Republicans on their philosophies about laws and government interventions. The general purpose of this study is to investigate a) if there is a difference in the percentage of students who were electronically bullied in Democrat states and Republican states and b) if there is a correlation between the percentage of students who were electronically bullied and the percentage of students who seriously considered suicide.  The results of the independent samples t-tests indicate that female high school students in Democrat states are less likely to be cyberbullied than in Republican states (although this did not apply to male students). The results of the linear regression analyses indicate that there is a positive relationship between the percentage of students who were cyberbullied and the percentage of students who seriously considered suicide.  Therefore, the problem of suicidal thoughts may be influenced through the control of cyberbullying. Cyberbullying can be controlled through appropriate laws supported by the political party.

# Table of Contents

# List of Tables

# List of Figures

# CHAPTER 1

## Introduction to the Problem

### Cyberbullying and Unguarded Teens

According to the Center for the Digital Future, the time that Americans spend on the Internet has increased dramatically in recent years (Lebo, 2010).  Evidently, electronic communications provide a new form of interaction that enables users to interact with other people more conveniently.  Indeed, the innovation of the Internet has benefited Americans in ways like never before. However, regardless of the conveniences, online interactions also have risks.  Because of the teenagers' increased use of social media, they are especially vulnerable to these risks.

Several studies suggest that teenagers are largely victimized by their Internet experiences (Kowalski, Limber & Agatston, 2012; Lenhart, 2009, 2010).  The use of social media with portable devices like cell phones, for instance, endangers teenagers, who often do not protect their personal information.  Predators steal their personal information from social media, which causes the teenagers harm.

Lenhart (2007) pointed out that 32% of teenagers have been cyberbullied.  Half of them reported being victimized due to the exposure of their private information without their permission.  Girls reported being the victim of cyberbullying more than boys.  Overall, cyberbullying is a serious and continuous problem among teenagers, which may lead to school problems, social problems, and mental health disorders (Lenhart, 2009).

According to Lenhart (2009, 2010), 75% of American teenagers in 2010 had cell phones, 63% of them spent time online every day, more than 93% of them used the Internet to surf online, and 89% of them surfed online from home.  According to this research, cell phone users received or sent an average of 50 text messages per day and one-third of them produced approximately 100 text messages every day.  Given these statistics, most teenagers are at risk of being harassed via technology.

**Figure 1. Computer crimes.**

## Partisanship and Cyberbullying

According to both the 2004 and the 2008 Uniform Crime Reports, Republican states had higher violent and property crime rates than did Democrat states (Ostermeier, 2009). The difference in the crime rates between the Democrat and Republican states may be attributed to several factors. For instance, Republican states were believed to be less wealthy than Democrat states. Out of all possible factors, however, legislative control and party policies have played a critical role in the difference in crime rates.

Figure 2. Partisanship.

Over the past decade, the government has responded to cyberbullying via legislation (Hinduja & Patchin, 2015). However, according to some studies, the Democrat Party tends to promote regulations that control cyberbullying while the Republican Party tends to oppose government regulations (Kneeland, 2016). Indeed, all fifty states, and Washington D. C., have passed bullying laws that include electronic harassment.

There have been debates over problems regarding bullying laws and policies (Hinduja & Patchin, 2015). First, although certain cyberbullying incidents may be dealt with federally, there is no federal anti-bullying law (Hinduja & Patchin, 2016). Second, although a few states have officially defined cyberbullying as an illegal offense, most states hand over authority to schools. Third, the schools cannot agree over the discipline of students' online behavior versus the students' civil rights. Additionally, although the schools are authorized to discipline students off campus when their speech or behavior causes serious school problems, the extent of punishment is controversial (Hinduja & Patchin, 2015).

**Figure 3. Laws.**

## Cyberbullying and Mental Health

The advancement of technology has increased social interactions between teens via social networks (Kowalski et al., 2012). However, the evidence suggests that frequent exposure to the Internet can cause serious problems. One study has found that there was a correlation between the amount of Internet use and levels of depression and feelings of loneliness (Kraut, Mukhopadhyay, Szczypula, Kiesler, & Scherlis, 1998). In addition, other studies suggest that both the victims and offenders of cyberbullying have shown signs of personality disorders, such as lower self-esteem, depression, and suicidal tendencies. As a result, those personality disorders may affect offline behaviors, which can cause serious problems in school and other social surroundings (Patchin & Hinduja, 2013).

## Deterrence Theory and its Limitations

The deterrence theory initially focused on the field of law and stressed the costs of legal sanctions (Liska & Messner, 1999). To discourage crime, the deterrence theory demands that the costs of crime be greater than the benefits gained from crime. Then it is a simple business decision. A person will decide not to commit a particular crime if the cost outweighs the benefit.

However, the deterrence theory relies on three factors: severity, certainty, and celerity of punishment (Liska & Messner, 1999). The severity of punishment stresses that the harshness of the punishment needs to be greater than the pleasures received from the crime. In other words, a slap on the wrist may not be enough to discourage a person from committing a million dollar crime. The certainty of punishment stresses that there needs to be a very good chance that an offender will get caught after committing a crime. In other words, a harsh punishment may not be enough to discourage crime if the offenders are never caught. Finally, the celerity of punishment stresses that punishment must be executed swiftly. In other words, getting caught and receiving a harsh punishment may not be enough to discourage crime if it takes 100 years for the offender to realize the punishment. In short, increasing the severity, certainty, and celerity of punishment can deter criminal behaviors.

In addition, there are two types of deterrence: specific and general (Liska & Messner, 1999). Specific deterrence emphasizes that the offender who is severely, certainly, and swiftly punished will be less likely to repeat crime. General deterrence emphasizes learning through observation. If residents see an offender who is severely, certainly, and swiftly apprehended and punished, then the observers will avoid committing crime due to the fear of being punished (Zimring, 1971;  Zimring & Hawkins, 1973).

**Figure 4. Certainty of punishment.**

The deterrence theory has limitations. First, the deterrence theory requires rational thought. In other words, the deterrence theory may be ineffective against those individuals who are unable to make a good business decision. Second, it is assumed that prison is punishment. For MS-13 gang members, for example, prison is not considered punishment (Poe, 2006). MS-13 gang members equate prison with universities, and those who are released back into society are considered to be graduates. Finally, if the three factors of deterrence (severity, certainty, and celerity) are not employed effectively and simultaneously, then the deterrence theory may actually promote crime (Liska & Messner, 1999). Of the three factors, celerity of punishment seems to be the most important.

**Figure 5. Celerity of punishment.**

# Statement of the Problem

Both Democrats and Republicans advocate Internet freedom and online privacy, yet they endorse different approaches for protecting online privacy and Internet freedom (Kenneth, 2012).  In addition, several researchers found that political orientation can influence social values (anti-social values or pro-social values) and psychological factors (Sheldon & Nichols, 2009; Sylwester & Purver, 2015).  Because youths use the Internet to bully other youths, these harsh electronic communications may cause serious harm.  Therefore, there is a need for further research for assessing the difference between political orientation and the rate of cyberbullying.

Some scholars state that there is a strong association between traditional bullying and suicide-related behaviors (Carney, 2000; Hertz, Donato, & Wright, 2013; Kim, Kon, & Lventhal, 2005; Roland, 2002).  Cyberbullying, a new type of bullying, has be linked to psychological problems, such as depression and loneliness (Kowalski et al., 2012; Kraut et al., 1998).   Cyberbullying has also been linked to behavioral problems, such as tobacco use, alcohol use, and poor school performance (Mitchell, Kiely, Miller, Connor, Spence, & Teno, 2007).   Therefore, it is logical to assume that cyberbullying may also be related to suicide-related behaviors.  Hence, it is necessary to evaluate the relationship between cyberbullying and suicidal thoughts.

**Figure 6. Cyberbullying.**

# Purpose of the Study

In consideration of the two parties' attitudes toward cyberbullying, this study has two main purposes. Although Republican states have higher violent and property crime rates than do Democrat states, the relationship between partisanship and cyberbullying is unclear (Kneeland, 2016; Ostermeier, 2009; U.S. Department of Justice, 2010). Therefore, the first purpose of this study is to determine whether there is a difference between Republican and Democrat states and the likelihood of being cyberbullied. This is important because they have different points of view on the laws relating to computer communications, which may influence the cyberbullying crime rates. The second purpose of this study is to determine if there is a relationship between the percentage of students who were cyberbullied and the percentage of students who seriously considered attempting suicide.

# Significance of the Study

Many incidents of cyberbullying have been reported by the public within the last decade (Kowalski et al., 2012). Some victims ended up committing suicide after they experienced cyberbullying (Vora, 2014). Megan Meier, for example, was one of the more infamous cases. Megan was an American teenage girl who committed suicide because she was harassed online by another female. Another high-profile case is Tyler Clementi, a high school graduate, who ended his life because his roommate shared information over the internet about Tyler's sexual orientation. Cyberbullying has not drawn the same amount of attention as other crimes, but it has already shown devastating effects on social safety and stability (Rivers & Duncan, 2013).

Cyberbullying and suicide are two social problems that require police investigation and can be reduced through the implementation of laws and policies. The results of this study may prove valuable to lawmakers, school administrators, and parents of school-age children. Policy-makers pass laws, school authorities enforce anti-bullying laws, and parents can choose where to live and raise a family.

Figure 7.  The law and deterrence theory.

# Research Design

This research study has utilized a quantitative correlational survey design.  A quantitative study provides the benefits of using numeric values and statistics to objectively analyze the relationship between the variables (Bordens & Abbott, 2008).  Furthermore, a correlational study allows for the prediction of the dependent variable based on the values of the independent variable (Leedy & Ormrod, 2005).

# Research Questions and Null Hypotheses

This study has examined a) the difference between Democrat and Republican states and the percentage of students who were electronically bullied, and b) the relationship between the percentage of students who were cyberbullied and the percentage of students who seriously considered attempting suicide.  Females and males were assessed separately and then jointly as a total group.

## Research Questions (RQ)

RQ1. Is there a difference between Democrat and Republican states and the percentage of female students who were electronically bullied?

RQ2. Is there a difference between Democrat and Republican states and the percentage of male students who were electronically bullied?

RQ3. Is there a difference between Democrat and Republican states and the total percentage of students who were electronically bullied?

RQ4. Is there a relationship between the percentage of female students who were cyberbullied and the percentage of female students who seriously considered attempting suicide?

RQ5.  Is there a relationship between the percentage of male students who were cyberbullied and the percentage of male students who seriously considered attempting suicide?

RQ6.  Is there a relationship between the total percentage of students who were cyberbullied and the total percentage of students who seriously considered attempting suicide?

## Null Hypotheses (HO)

HO1. There is no difference between Democrat and Republican states and the percentage of female students who were electronically bullied.

HO2. There is no difference between Democrat and Republican states and the percentage of male students who were electronically bullied.

HO3. There is no difference between Democrat and Republican states and the total percentage of students who were electronically bullied.

HO4. There is no relationship between the percentage of female students who were cyberbullied and the percentage of female students who seriously considered attempting suicide.

HO5. There is no relationship between the percentage of male students who were cyberbullied and the percentage of male students who seriously considered attempting suicide.

HO6. There is no relationship between the total percentage of students who were cyberbullied and the total percentage of students who seriously considered attempting suicide.

# Assumptions and Limitations

There are several assumptions in this study. First, the researcher assumes that the participants who responded to the surveys were truthful and forthcoming. Second, the researcher assumes that respondents are the individuals who completed the surveys. Third, the researcher assumes that a red state (i.e., Republican state) will be in alignment with the Republican Party's paradigm and a blue state (i.e., Democrat state) will be in alignment with the Democrat party's paradigm. There is a difference between the Democrat paradigm and Republican paradigm on laws and government interventions (Deffen, n.d., Kenneth, 2012; Kneeland, 2016). Because the President is the chief law enforcement officer in the United States, and because he has the authority to influence law enforcement efforts, the partisanship that a particular state supports during the Presidential election indicates the paradigm that the state supports. Thus, when a state votes Republican or Democrat during the Presidential election, that state may influence law enforcement efforts. Finally, because laws may impact behaviors, it is assumed that the participants are impacted in the same way by the same laws.

There are several limitations in this study. First, because the study has a correlational design, it does not reflect causal relationships (Bordens & Abbott, 2008). Second, because the sample is limited to school students in grades 9 - 12, the findings cannot be generalized to other populations (Eaton et al., 2012; Kann et al., 2014; Kann et al., 2016). Third, because many crimes are not reported to the police, the data used in this study may be incomplete (Centers for Disease Control and Prevention, 2014). Fourth, because cyberbullying is a recent problem, there are only 3 years of data available (2011, 2013, and 2015). Thus, the amount of available data is less than optimal. Fifth, because the data used in the study are second-hand and collected for a different reason, the data values cannot be more clearly defined (Denscombe, 2007). Finally, because the study is quantitative in nature, it does not provide an in-depth understanding of the meanings that the participants have associated with their lived experiences (Berg, 2007).

Figure 8. Presidential election and partisanship.

# Operational Definition of Terms

*Cyberbullying.* Cyberbullying, also called electronic bullying, refers to people using electronic communication platforms to harass, embarrass, or threaten others (Kowalski et al., 2012).

*Republican (red) and Democrat (blue) state.* Each state was classified as Republican or Democrat by how the state voted on prior Presidential elections. This study uses survey data from 2011, 2013, and 2015. Therefore, each state's partisanship classification for the 2011 data set was based on the state's 2008 Presidential election. Likewise, each state's partisanship classification for the 2013 data set and 2015 data set was based on the state's 2012 Presidential election. Only states that voted consistently Democrat or consistently Republican in the 2008 and 2012 Presidential elections were considered.

# Expected Findings

Republican and Democrat parties have endorsed different approaches to Internet freedom and to the privacy of information in their party platforms (Kenneth, 2012). In addition, some research studies indicate that political orientation can influence psychological factors and social values (anti-social values or pro-social values) (Sheldon, & Nichols, 2009; Sylwester, & Purver, 2015). Thus, the researcher expects that there will be a difference between partisanship and cyberbullying.

Some studies indicate that teenagers who have been cyberbullied are highly likely to have suicidal thoughts (Allison, & William, 2012; Hinduja & Patchin, 2010). Therefore, the researcher expects that there will be a positive relationship between being cyberbullied and having suicidal thoughts.

# Summary

This study examines a) if there is a difference in the percentage of cyberbullying between Republican and Democrat states and b) if there is a relationship between being cyberbullied and having suicidal thoughts. Chapter one describes cyberbullying and related problems, the theoretical framework, the significance of the study, the research design, the research questions, the study's assumptions and limitations, and expected findings. Chapter 2 presents a literature review on political orientation and cyberbullying. Chapter 3 discusses the current study's methodology. Chapter 4 analyzes the current study's data. Finally, Chapter 5 describes the current study's results.

# CHAPTER 2

## Introduction

The purpose of the current study is to examine a) the difference between Republican and Democrat states and the percentage of students who were electronically bullied, and b) the relationship between the percentage of students who were electronically bullied and the percentage of students who seriously considered attempting suicide. First, if there is a relationship between cyberbullying and suicidal tendencies, then the control of cyberbullying must be taken into consideration. Second, several studies illustrate that political orientation correlates to social behavior and psychological factors (Sheldon & Nichols, 2009; Sylwester & Purver, 2015). Thus, regarding their different attitudes toward the control of cyberbullying, the two parties may make a different contribution to cyberbullying rates.

**Figure 9. Electronic bullying is a crime.**

The deterrence theory claims that the high cost of legal sanctions will reduce the incentives to commit crime (Liska & Messner, 1999). This will be true if the costs for crime outweigh the benefits gained from gain. The deterrence theory has three factors and all must be effectively employed: certainty, severity, and celerity of punishment. Each of these factors must be sufficiently high to effectively realize the benefits of the deterrence theory. Regarding political orientation, cyberbullying, and suicidal thoughts, the deterrence theory may provide an effective way for the government, school districts, and educators to reduce cyberbullying incidents.

Because academic research is built upon prior studies, it is important to review the current literature. Thus, prior studies that involve the current study's theory and variables have been reviewed. The review of the literature includes a) Twitter language use and psychological differences between Democrats and Republicans, b) coping of cyberbullying victims among college students, c) bullying, cyberbullying, and suicide, and d) bullying in school and cyberspace.

**Figure 10. Punishment for youth.**

# Theoretical Orientation

## Deterrence Theory

According to the deterrence theory, it is believed that individuals will freely and logically choose to obey the law if the costs for violating the law are greater than the benefits gained from violating the law (Akers & Sellers, 2009; Liska & Messner, 1999). The deterrence theory relies on three factors: severity of punishment, certainty of punishment, and celerity of punishment. The severity of punishment relies on harsh consequences to reduce the temptation of committing crime. The certainty of punishment provides maximum possibility of arrest and punishment of crime offenders. The celerity of punishment stresses that the criminals must be sanctioned swiftly and effectively once they commit the crime. In short, the greater the severity, certainty, and celerity of punishment, the greater an individual's fear of engaging in criminal behavior. This theory can be utilized by legislators and political parties by passing laws that influence the severity, certainty, and celerity of punishment (Akers & Sellers, 2009).

The deterrence theory has two aspects: specific deterrence and general deterrence (Zimring, 1971; Zimring & Hawkins, 1973). Specific deterrence emphasizes that an offender who is severely, certainly, and swiftly punished will learn through personal experience not to engage in crime. The offender will personally experience the high cost of crime. General deterrence is realized when the general public learns through observation the high cost of crime. The general public will avoid committing crime in fear of being punished like the offender.

## Theoretical Criticisms

The deterrence theory has several limitations (Davis, 2015). First, the deterrence theory is based rational thought. In other words, the deterrence theory may be ineffective against those individuals who are unable to make a good business decision. Second, the deterrence theory overemphasizes the importance of individual choice while discounting emotions and social factors, such as poverty. Third, it is assumed that a prison sentence is punishment. However, for MS-13 gang members, for example, serving time in prison is not considered punishment (Poe, 2006). MS-13 gang members equate serving time in prison with attending a university, which is a reward. Fourth, the deterrence theory includes three core factors: severity, certainty, and celerity of punishment (Liska & Messner, 1999). However, if all three factors are not effectively implemented, then the deterrence theory may actually promote crime. For example, when the police department cannot ensure the apprehension of offenders, or the criminal system fails to provide the certain legal penalties for offenders, then individuals may believe that the benefits of crime outweigh the costs of crime.

**Figure 11. Tough on crime.**

## Validation of Deterrence Theory

Studies conducted by Gibbs (1968), Tittle (1969), and Chiricos and Waldo (1970) examined the effect of certainty and severity of punishment as deterrents for crime. However, the celerity of punishment was not assessed in the studies and has been seldom included in the past studies (Nagin & Pogarsky, 2001). The researchers measured the certainty and severity of punishment with objective and perceptual measures of deterrence. Regarding the objective measure of deterrence, the certainty of punishment was measured by the percentage of offenders who were arrested and prosecuted. In addition, the severity of punishment was measured by the average length of punishment for a specific crime. The perceptual measure of deterrence examined how well citizens understand the legal penalties. In other words, the researchers assessed how the citizens' perceptions of punishment affected their decisions whether or not to commit crime. The researchers found that there was a negative correlation between certainty of punishment and criminal behavior with both objective and perceptual measures of deterrence, but the correlation was very weak. However, the severity of punishment was seldom found to deter crime.

Legal sanctions involving arrest and punishment are believed to be the cores in reducing crime (Akers & Sellers, 2009). Based on legislation, law enforcement officers identify certain acts as illegal and start the punishment process on offenders. According to the deterrence theory, severity, certainty, and celerity of punishments can effectively reduce crime through both general and specific deterrence. Indeed, the deterrence theory has played a significant role in the entire criminal justice system.

Figure 12. Severity of punishment.

# Current Problems and Possible Solutions

The epidemic of cyberbullying has resulted in numerous anti-bullying laws within the last decade (Hinduja & Patchin, 2015). Most states, as well as Washington D. C., have enacted anti-bullying laws that include electronic harassment. However, only 26 states define the exact word cyberbullying in the law. It is worth noting that there are some concerns with the current anti-bullying laws and policies (Hinduja & Patchin, 2015). First and foremost, although some cyberbullying incidents may be dealt with at the federal level, there is no federal anti-bullying law (Hinduja & Patchin, 2016). Second, only a few states formally define cyberbullying as an illegal offense and specify sanctions for the criminal conduct. Most legislative departments hand over the authority to schools; that is, the regulation and discipline of teenagers' cyberbullying behaviors are restricted to school districts. Third, there is a continual debate among schools between the discipline of students' online behavior and the violation of civil rights. In addition, although the schools are authorized to discipline students off campus when their speech or behaviors cause serious school problems, the extent of enforcement for educators is controversial (Hinduja & Patchin, 2015).

The deterrence theory has three factors: severity, certainty and celerity of punishment. Because the partisanship of a state indicates its paradigm on law enforcement efforts and punishment, partisanship will influence cyberbullying crimes. The U.S. President is the chief federal law enforcement officer in the country and has a large budget, which can be allocated to combat cyberbullying. Therefore, the people's choice of partisanship for the U.S. Presidency will affect cyberbullying laws, which may affect the number of suicidal thoughts. Indeed, U.S. law enforcement promotes public service and safety. Cyberbullying and suicide are two social problems that require law enforcement intervention and can be reduced through the implementation of the deterrence theory.

According to the deterrence theory, crime can be reduced by increasing the cost of legal sanctions (Liska & Messner, 1999). Thus, there are several possible solutions that may reduce cyberbullying. First, the legislators could establish more comprehensive anti-bullying laws. For instance, the term cyberbullying should be clearly defined. State anti-bullying laws need to specify the exact sanctions for this behavior. Second, the legislative departments should complement and improve the database of cyberbullying litigation. One of the factors that has undermined the scare tactics of the deterrence theory is that many bullying lawsuits have been resolved out of court (Kowalski et al., 2012). Thus, the scholars lack data for research and the public may underestimate the seriousness of cyberbullying. Third, as the legislative departments make it clear that schools districts have enforcement authority over the issue of cyberbullying, the schools should be responsible for the students' behavior.

However, the schools disagree over the discipline of students' cyberbullying behavior and about U.S. constitutional rights (Kowalski et al, 2012). Therefore, legislators may need to define and provide the laws that govern the schools' regulation over students' words and behaviors. Fourth, educators and school personnel do not only have the duty to discipline the cyberbullies, but they also have the responsibility to care about the victims' mental health (Hinduja & Patchin, 2015). Thus, educators and school personnel may need to supply long-term training programs for cyberbullying prevention and remedy.

# Review of the Literature

Academic research builds upon prior studies. Thus, it is important to review prior studies. The following is a review of the published literature, which discusses political orientation, language use, emotional expression, social values, cyberbullying, depressive symptoms, and suicidal thoughts.

## Twitter language use and psychological differences between Democrats and Republicans

Sylwester and Purver (2015) undertook a qualitative study to examine the different language usages and ways of expression on Twitter between users with different political orientations (liberals & conservatives). The samples were solicited from the official Twitter accounts of the Republican and Democrat U.S. Congressional Parties. It involved 5,375 followers from three American Democrat Twitter accounts and 5,386 followers from three Republican Twitter accounts. Data were collected in June 2014. There was no content restriction in the process; that is, it included all the words, behaviors, and interests of users. The process of the analysis included three parts: a) it described how Twitter users interacted; b) it examined the most distinguished words of the two groups; and c) it predicted the political orientation based on the Linguistic Inquiry and Word Count (LIWC). LIWC consisted of many dictionaries that described different kinds of categories or words. This study indicated that the users of Democrat accounts were more likely to swear and use hate-related words, which may be against the law, than did the users of Republican accounts.

However, the study does have several limitations. First, Twitter was used as the data source and some Twitter messages were posted by institutions and not by individuals, which means the content of the messages were possibly deliberately designed (Sylwester & Purver, 2015). Second, the analysis was based only on simple words and the analysis cannot ensure actual meanings. For example, the researchers did not take all punctuations and emotions into consideration.

## Cyberbullying behaviors among college students

Schenk and Fremouw (2012) performed a study to explore the emotional distress caused by cyberbullying behaviors among college students. A total of 799 college students, comprised of 71.6% females and 28.4% males who were 18 to 24 years of age, were divided into victim and control groups. They were asked to complete a questionnaire that combined a couple of questionnaires from previous cyberbullying studies. The researchers used an independent samples t-test and found that the victim group had higher levels of psychological symptoms, such as anxiety and depression, than the control group. However, there was little difference between males and females.

There are some limitations in this study. First, Schenk and Fremouw (2012) studied college students, which may not apply to the present study, which examines high school students. Second, because the data are based on self-reports, the results may be less than completely truthful.

## Bullying in school and cyberspace

Perren, Dooley, Shaw, and Cross (2010) conducted a study to examine if the victims who were cyberbullied had the same negative symptoms as the victims of traditional bullying. The data from participants were collected from both Australia and Switzerland. A sample of 1,694 adolescents were chosen from schools of the two countries. The participants were asked to finish a survey that identified them as perpetrators or victims, which included depression scales and negative symptoms. The researchers applied tobit regressions in the data analysis, and the findings indicated that the victims of cyberbullying were more likely to exhibit depressive symptoms.

However, there are some limitations in this study. First, all participants of Australia were chosen from religious-affiliated schools (Perren et al.,

2010).  It is unclear if religious students are different in a meaningful way from non-religious students.  Second, the data were collected from participants in Australia and Switzerland, which may not represent the population in the present study, which examines participants in America. In other words, the findings of the study may not be applied to other populations that do not match the sample's characteristics (i.e., external validity issues).

**Figure 13. The reach of cyberspace.**

## Bullying, cyberbullying and suicide

Hinduja and Patchin (2010) conducted a study to determine if cyberbullying victims have suicidal thoughts. The data were collected during the spring of 2007. Almost 2,000 students from 30 middle schools in the United States participated in the survey. They were asked a large number of questions that involved being bullied both online and offline, and if they had thoughts of attempting suicide after being bullied. The researchers performed logistic regression analysis and the findings indicated that the juveniles who were cyberbullied were more likely to consider suicide. There was no difference between female and male victims.

However, the study also suffers from some limitations. First, because the data were collected within one year, it is difficult to determine incremental changes over a long period of time (Brownfield & Sorenson, 1993). Second, it was a self-report study, which means there is a possibility that the participants reported what they perceived was important to society rather than what really happened.

# Synthesis of the Research Findings

In reviewing the literature, several variables have been examined, which include the following: political orientation, language use, emotional expression, social values, cyberbullying, depressive symptoms, and suicidal thoughts. First, the evidence indicates that personal political orientation is related to language use, emotional expression, and social values. In addition, several studies suggest that cyberbullying contributes to psychological problems and suicidal thoughts.

# Summary of Literature Review

In regards to the past studies, several issues are worth mentioning. First, Twitter users of Democrat accounts are more likely to use hate speech on the computer than Twitter users of Republican accounts (Sylwester & Purver, 2015). Second, cyberbullying causes emotional distress, such as anxiety and depression. Finally, the victims of cyberbullying are more likely to consider suicide.

However, there is a gap in knowledge involving cyberbullying behavior, political orientation, and suicidal thoughts. The deterrence theory is a tool that can be manipulated to reduce crime, if implemented properly. Thus, this study can provide valuable information that may be useful to legislators, school educators, and parents to help deal with the serious issue of cyberbullying.

# CHAPTER 3

## METHODOLOGY

## Purpose of the Study

The political attitudes of Republican and Democrat parties are different on the government's intervention on cyberbullying (Deffen, n.d.; Kenneth, 2012; Kneeland, 2016). Thus, party affiliation may play a role in the outcome of cyberbullying rates. In addition, the frequent use of the Internet may increase the risk of negative emotions. For instance, people who are seriously abused and harassed via the Internet tend to have suicidal thoughts (Kraut et al., 1998). Furthermore, although there are some studies that examine the relationship between cyberbullying and suicidal thoughts, and between political preference and social value orientation, there is little research involving political party, cyberbullying, and suicidal thoughts (Allison, & William, 2012; Hinduja & Patchin, 2010; Van Lange, Bekkers, Chirumbolo, & Leone, 2012). Therefore, in order to fill in the gap in knowledge, this study examines a) party affiliation and the percentage of students who are cyberbullied and b) the relationship between the percentage of students who are cyberbullied and the percentage of students who have suicidal thoughts.

## Research Design

This research study utilized a quantitative correlational survey design. A quantitative study provides the benefits of using numeric values and statistics to objectively analyze the relationship between the variables (Bordens & Abbott, 2008). Indeed, a quantitative study was required to answer the research questions. Second, correlational studies are most effective for predicting the values of the dependent variable based upon the known values of the independent variables (Leedy & Ormrod, 2005). Finally, surveys efficiently collect a large amount of information in a uniform manner (Champion, 2006).

## Target Population and Participant Selection

The target population for the current study consisted of students in grades 9–12, who attended public and private schools in the United States. Female students and male students were assessed separately and then jointly as a total group.

# Procedures

This study examined electronic government-based second-hand data gathered from the Youth Risk Behavior Surveillance System (YRBSS) in 2011, 2013 and 2015 (Eaton et al., 2012; Kann et al., 2014; Kann et al., 2016). The data were collected by the Centers for Disease Control and Prevention, which is devoted to the public's safety and health. A three-stage cluster sample design produced a nationally representative sample of students in grades 9–12, who attended public and private schools. Because the sampling frames for the three surveys were not the same, and because it is likely that the students who were randomly sampled at the third stage of each study were different for each study, the data retrieved from 2011, 2013, and 2015 were considered independent, which is a parametric assumption (Su, 2017). There were 78 total data values collected and examined.

## Percentage Values as Data

The data values were collected from various states in the United States as a) the percentage of students who were cyberbullied and b) the percentage of students who seriously considered attempting suicide. It is less of an issue that the variables are expressed as percentage values than the underlying distribution of the variables and the residuals of linear regression (Long, 1997; Peng & Davis, 2017a; Su, 2017). Because the research questions involving cyberbullying and suicidal thoughts plan to utilize linear regression, if the percentage data values are to be used as given, then the parametric assumptions for linear regression will need to be satisfied. If the percentage values are not normally distributed, then the data may need to be transformed (e.g., logit or arcsine transformation) or a nonparametric statistic may need to be used. This will be addressed in the data analysis section.

# Measures

The State Youth Risk Behavior Survey (YRBS) collects data on health and life-threatening problems among students in the United States (Eaton et al., 2012; Kann et al., 2014; Kann et al., 2016). The youth-based state survey was conducted by state and local education and health organizations within public and private school districts. The standard questionnaire in 2011 and 2013 included 86 questions; the standard questionnaire in 2015 consisted of 89 questions. The state surveys may have been modified slightly by adding or deleting certain questions. All participants voluntarily completed the self-administered Youth Risk Behavior Survey during one class period by recording their responses directly onto an answer sheet. In order to protect the participants' privacy, surveys across states were conducted with anonymity.

## Reliability of the Youth Risk Behavior Survey Questionnaire (YRBS)

This standard questionnaire has been shown to be reliable (Brener, Kann, McManus, Kinchen, Sundberg, & Ross, 2002). The Youth Risk Behavior Surveillance standard questionnaire was based on a range of health problems existing in national, state, and large urban schools. The test-retest method was used to examine the reliability of Youth Risk Behavior Survey questionnaire. A total of 4,916 female and male high school students from different grade levels and ethnicities completed the survey twice, two weeks apart. A Kappa statistic, which compares an observed accuracy with an expected accuracy, was computed to compare the group prevalence estimates for each risk factor at both test times. Although twenty-two percent of items had significantly different prevalence estimates between the two test times, overall, the students seemed to report health risks behaviors consistent over time. Furthermore, there were no differences between genders, grades, and races. As a result, the Youth Risk Behavior Survey questionnaire has shown to be reliable. However, additional tests are required to demonstrate the survey's validity.

# Research Questions and Null Hypotheses

The research questions examine the influence of party affiliation on cyberbullying and cyberbullying-related suicidal thoughts. This study examined a) the difference between Democrat and Republican states and the percentage of students who were electronically bullied, and b) the relationship between the percentage of students who were cyberbullied and the percentage of students who seriously considered attempting suicide. Female students and male students were assessed separately and then jointly as a total group.

## Research Questions (RQ)
RQ1. Is there a difference between Democrat and Republican states and the percentage of female students who were electronically bullied?

RQ2. Is there a difference between Democrat and Republican states and the percentage of male students who were electronically bullied?

RQ3. Is there a difference between Democrat and Republican states and the total percentage of students who were electronically bullied?

RQ4. Is there a relationship between the percentage of female students who were cyberbullied and the percentage of female students who seriously considered attempting suicide?

RQ5.  Is there a relationship between the percentage of male students who were cyberbullied and the percentage of male students who seriously considered attempting suicide?

RQ6.  Is there a relationship between the total percentage of students who were cyberbullied and the total percentage of students who seriously considered attempting suicide?

## Null Hypotheses (HO)

HO1.  There is no difference between Democrat and Republican states and the percentage of female students who were electronically bullied.

HO2.  There is no difference between Democrat and Republican states and the percentage of male students who were electronically bullied.

HO3.  There is no difference between Democrat and Republican states and the total percentage of students who were electronically bullied.

HO4.  There is no relationship between the percentage of female students who were cyberbullied and the percentage of female students who seriously considered attempting suicide.

HO5.  There is no relationship between the percentage of male students who were cyberbullied and the percentage of male students who seriously considered attempting suicide.

HO6.  There is no relationship between the total percentage of students who were cyberbullied and the total percentage of students who seriously considered attempting suicide.

# Data Analysis Procedures

The study used the Statistical Package for Social Sciences (SPSS) to examine a) the difference between Democrat and Republican states and the percentage of students who were electronically bullied, and b) the relationship between the percentage of students who were cyberbullied and the percentage of students who seriously considered attempting suicide.  The independent samples t-test was used to assess the difference between political party and the percentage of students who were electronically bullied.  The independent samples t-test was applied to HO1 - HO3.  Linear regression analysis was used to assess the relationship between the percentage of students who were cyberbullied and the percentage of students who seriously considered attempting suicide.  Linear regression was applied to HO4 - HO6.

## Independent Samples t-test

The independent samples t-test is an inferential statistic that determines whether the difference in the means of two groups is unlikely to have occurred because of random chance (Lunenburg & Irby, 2007). For this test, it is important that the data values are independent (i.e., the same person did not complete more than one survey) (Norusis, 2012). As stated earlier, because the sampling frames for the three surveys were not the same, and because it is likely that the students who were randomly sampled at the third stage of each study were different for each study, the data values retrieved from 2011, 2013, and 2015 are considered independent (Su, 2017).

## Linear Regression

Linear regression is an inferential statistic that is used to determine the relationship between two continuous variables (Lunenburg & Irby, 2007; Norusis, 2012). If the value of the independent variable is known, then the value of the dependent variable can be predicted. However, it is important to check that the parametric assumptions have been satisfied. If the parametric assumptions have not been satisfied, then the data may need to be transformed so that the assumptions are satisfied or a nonparametric statistic may need to be used.

# Expected Findings

Republican and Democrat parties have endorsed different approaches to Internet freedom and to the privacy of information in their party platforms (Kenneth, 2012). In addition, some research studies indicate that political orientation can influence psychological factors and social value preferences (anti-social values or pro-social values) (Sheldon, & Nichols, 2009; Sylwester, & Purver, 2015). Thus, the researcher expects that there will be a difference between political party and cyberbullying.

Some studies indicate that teenagers who have been cyberbullied are very likely to have suicidal thoughts (Allison, & William, 2012; Hinduja & Patchin, 2010). Therefore, the researcher expects that there will be a positive relationship between being cyberbullied and having suicidal thoughts.

The deterrence theory depends on three factors: severity, certainty, and celerity of punishment (Liska & Messner, 1999). Because cyberbullying and suicidal thoughts are two social problems that should be reduced by the government, the government can use the deterrence theory to manage these two issues.

# CHAPTER 4

## DATA COLLECTION & ANALYSIS OF FINDINGS

## Introduction

The purpose of this study was to assess the difference between Republican and Democrat states and being cyberbullied. In addition, this study determined if there was a correlation between being electronically bullied and suicidal thoughts. The study utilized the electronic government-based second-hand data from the Youth Risk Behavior Surveillance System. This chapter presents the findings of the stated research questions.

The deterrence theory suggests that crime can be reduced by increasing the severity, certainty, and celerity of punishment (Liska & Messner, 1999). Because the Democrat paradigm differs from the Republican paradigm on laws and intervention, the partisanship of the government will influence law enforcement efforts on cyberbullying. Furthermore, cyberbullying laws may impact the number of suicidal thoughts.

For research questions 1-3, political party is the independent variable (IV) and being cyberbullied in the dependent variable (DV). For research questions 4-6, being cyberbullied in the independent variable (IV) and having suicidal thoughts is the dependent variable (DV). To control for gender, females and males were assessed separately and then jointly as a total group.

## Research Questions and Null Hypotheses

Statistical analyses were performed in this study to examine a) if there is a difference in political party affiliation and the amount of cyberbullying, and b) if there is a relationship between being cyberbullied and having suicidal thoughts. The independent samples t-test was used to examine the difference between Democrat and Republican states and the percentage of students who were electronically bullied. In addition, linear regression was used to assess the relationship between the percentage of students who were cyberbullied and the percentage of students who seriously considered attempting suicide. Males and females were assessed separately and then jointly as a total group. The following research questions guided this study.

### Research Questions (RQ)

RQ1. Is there a difference between Democrat and Republican states and the percentage of female students who were electronically bullied?

RQ2. Is there a difference between Democrat and Republican states and the percentage of male students who were electronically bullied?

RQ3. Is there a difference between Democrat and Republican states and the total percentage of students who were electronically bullied?

RQ4. Is there a relationship between the percentage of female students who were cyberbullied and the percentage of female students who seriously considered attempting suicide?

RQ5. Is there a relationship between the percentage of male students who were cyberbullied and the percentage of male students who seriously considered attempting suicide?

RQ6. Is there a relationship between the total percentage of students who were cyberbullied and the total percentage of students who seriously considered attempting suicide?

## Null Hypotheses (HO)

HO1. There is no difference between Democrat and Republican states and the percentage of female students who were electronically bullied.

HO2. There is no difference between Democrat and Republican states and the percentage of male students who were electronically bullied.

HO3. There is no difference between Democrat and Republican states and the total percentage of students who were electronically bullied.

HO4. There is no relationship between the percentage of female students who were cyberbullied and the percentage of female students who seriously considered attempting suicide.

HO5. There is no relationship between the percentage of male students who were cyberbullied and the percentage of male students who seriously considered attempting suicide.

HO6. There is no relationship between the total percentage of students who were cyberbullied and the total percentage of students who seriously considered attempting suicide.

# Data Analysis Strategy and Organization of Statistical Results

The study used the electronic government-based second-hand data from the Youth Risk Behavior Surveillance System in 2011, 2013 and 2015 (Eaton et al., 2012; Kann et al., 2014; Kann et al., 2016). The data were entered into SPSS Version 22.0. Next, descriptive statistics were conducted to check whether the assumptions of the parametric statistics were satisfied (Norusis, 2012). Finally, three independent samples t-tests were employed to assess HO1 - HO3 and to assess HO4 - HO6 and to answer RQ4 - RQ6.

The results of this study are presented in three steps. First, the sample and source of the data are described. Second, descriptive statistics and the normality of the data are discussed. Finally, the results of the parametric statistics are presented, which allow the research questions to be answered.

# Description of the Sample

This study examined electronic government-based second-hand data gathered from the Youth Risk Behavior Surveillance System (YRBSS) in 2011, 2013 and 2015 (Eaton et al., 2012; Kann et al., 2014; Kann et al., 2016). The data were collected by the Centers for Disease Control and Prevention, which is devoted to the public's safety and health. A three-stage cluster sample design produced a nationally representative sample of students in grades 9–12, who attended public and private schools.

# Descriptive Statistics & Parametric Assumptions

The data were imported into SPSS Version 22.0. Subsequently, descriptive statistics and exploratory analysis were performed on the data to provide an overview of the general nature of the data and to assess whether the parametric assumptions have been satisfied (Norusis, 2008). To check the data's pattern of distribution, the researcher developed plots for electronic bullying and suicidal thoughts that consisted of the following: stem-and-leaf plot, histogram, boxplot, and Q-Q plot. The plots indicate that the data are close to normal. See Appendix.

## Percentage Values

As stated earlier, it is less of an issue that the variables are expressed as percentage values than the underlying distribution of the variables and the residuals of linear regression (Long, 1997; Su, 2017). In other words, if the data are normally distributed and if the parametric assumptions for linear regression are satisfied, then the percentage values can be used without transformation. Thus, before linear regression can be applied to the data, the model's assumptions need to be assessed.

## Linear Regression Assumptions

Linear regression is a parametric statistic and is useful for determining the relationships between variables. For linear regression, the model assumptions are 1) independence (independent observations), 2)

normality (residuals are normally distributed), 3) homoscedasticity (residuals have constant variance),
and 4) linearity (linear relationship between the independent and dependent variables) (Norusis, 2012; Su, 2017).

First, the independence assumption was checked using the Durbin–Watson statistic, which was 1.589 for females and 1.780 for males (See Appendix). A value of the Durbin–Watson statistic between 1.5 and 2.5 suggests the independence assumption holds true (Norusis, 2012; Su, 2017). Second, the Shapiro-Wilk normality test and the Q-Q plot of Studentized residuals were used to determine if the data are normally distributed. The p-values of the Shapiro-Wilk tests for females ($p = 0.124$) and males ($p = 0.862$) were greater than 0.05, which indicate that the data are normally distributed. The normality of data was also confirmed by the Q-Q plot of Studentized residuals. Because most of the data cluster around a straight line, this indicates that the distribution of the residuals is close to normal. Third, the homoscedasticity assumption was checked with Studentized Residuals versus Predicted Values plots. The plots indicate that the variance of suicidal thoughts is constant across electronic bullying (there were no recognizable patterns in the plots for females, males, and total). Finally, scatter plots and lines-of-best fit indicate that there is a linear relationship between the independent and dependent variables. Thus, the parametric assumptions were satisfied and linear regression can be used on the data values.

## Independent Samples *t-test*

There were 36 data values for the Democrat states and 42 values for the Republican states. The Democrat states mean for percent bullied females was 20.53 (SD = 3.58) and the Republican states mean was 22.55 (SD = 3.44). The Democrat states mean for percent bullied males was 10.88 (SD = 1.84) and the Republican states mean was 10.48 (SD = 1.83). The Democrat states mean for total percent bullied was 15.69 (SD = 2.50) and the Republican states mean was 16.42 (SD = 2.23).
See *Table 1* for an overview of the descriptive statistics for partisanship and cyberbullying.

Table 1

*Descriptive Statistics of Sample: Female, Male, and Total Students*

**Females:** *Descriptive Statistics for Partisanship and Electronically Bullied*

**Partisanship and Electronically Bullied - % Female Students**

Dependent Variable: Electronically Bullied (Females)

++++++++++++++++++++++++++++++++++++++++++++++++++++++++

|            | N  | Mean   | SD    | SE    |
|------------|----|--------|-------|-------|
| Democrat   | 36 | 20.527 | 3.582 | .5971 |
| Republican | 42 | 22.547 | 3.442 | .5312 |

++++++++++++++++++++++++++++++++++++++++++++++++++++++++

**Males:** *Descriptive Statistics for Partisanship and Electronically Bullied*

**Partisanship and Electronically Bullied - % Male Students**

Dependent Variable: Electronically Bullied (Males)

++++++++++++++++++++++++++++++++++++++++++++++++++++++++

|            | N  | Mean   | SD    | SE    |
|------------|----|--------|-------|-------|
| Democrat   | 36 | 10.877 | 1.843 | .3072 |
| Republican | 42 | 10.483 | 1.833 | .2829 |

++++++++++++++++++++++++++++++++++++++++++++++++++++++++

**Total:** *Descriptive Statistics for Partisan States and Electronically Bullied*

**Partisanship and Electronically Bullied – % Total Students**

Dependent Variable: Electronically Bullied (Total)

++++++++++++++++++++++++++++++++++++++++++++++++++++++++

|            | N  | Mean   | SD    | SE    |
|------------|----|--------|-------|-------|
| Democrat   | 36 | 15.688 | 2.496 | .4161 |
| Republican | 42 | 16.421 | 2.229 | .3440 |

++++++++++++++++++++++++++++++++++++++++++++++++++++++++

# Details of Analysis and Results

The current study used the independent samples t-test to determine the difference between Republican and Democrat states and cyberbullying; linear regression was used to determine the relationship between cyberbullying and suicidal thoughts. The independent samples t-test is effective for comparing the means of two independent groups (samples) in order to determine whether there is statistical evidence that the associated population means are significantly different (Lunenburg & Irby, 2007). Linear regression is effective for modeling the relationship between two continuous variables (Norusis, 2012).

## Independent Samples *t*-Test – Partisanship and Females

An independent samples t-test was performed to compare female students who were electronically bullied in Democrat (1) states and in Republican (2) states. See Table 2. The Levene's test is not significant; therefore, equal variances are assumed. Because the researcher is uncertain which political party, if any, will influence electronic bullying, a two-tailed test has been employed.

# Table 2
*T-test Results: Partisanship and Female Students*

## Dependent Variable: Females Being Cyberbullied

+++++++++++++++++++++++++++++++++++++++++++++++++++++++++++

|  | N | Mean | SD | SE |
|---|---|---|---|---|
| Democrat State | 36 | 20.527 | 3.582 | .5971 |
| Republican State | 42 | 22.547 | 3.442 | .5312 |

+++++++++++++++++++++++++++++++++++++++++++++++++++++++++++

## Partisanship and Females Being Cyberbullied

Levene's test is not significant; therefore, equal variances are assumed.

## Dependent Variable: Cyberbullied Females

+++++++++++++++++++++++++++++++++++++++++++++++++++++++++++

|  | Levene's test for Equality of Variance | | | | Sig. |
|---|---|---|---|---|---|
|  | F | Sig | t | df | (2-tailed) |

+++++++++++++++++++++++++++++++++++++++++++++++++++++++++++

| **Equal Variances Assumed** | .135 | .714 | -2.535 | 76 | .013* |
| Equal variances not Assumed | | | -2.527 | 73.19 | .014* |

+++++++++++++++++++++++++++++++++++++++++++++++++++++++++++

**significant at p<.05*

## Summary of Democrat states (1) and Republican states (2)

M1 = 20.527, SD1 = 3.582, SE1 = .5971

M2 = 22.547, SD2 = 3.442, SE2 = .5312

$t$ (76) = -2.535, p < .05, two-tailed

As expected, there was a significant difference in the percentage of female students who were electronically bullied between Democrat states and Republican states. Female students who were electronically bullied in Republican states displayed a higher mean

(M2 = 22.547, SD2 = 3.442, SE2 = .5312) than in Democrat states

(M1 = 20.527, SD1 = 3.582, SE1 = .5971); p < .05, two-tailed.

## Independent Samples t-test – Partisanship and Males

An independent samples t-test was performed to compare male students who were electronically bullied (EBM) in Democrat (1) states and in Republican (2) states. See Table 3. The Levene's test is not significant; therefore, equal variances are assumed. Because the researcher is uncertain which political party, if any, will influence electronic bullying, a two-tailed test has been employed.

Table 3
*T-test Results: Partisanship and Male Students*


**Dependent Variable: Males Being Cyberbullied**
++++++++++++++++++++++++++++++++++++++++++++++++++++++++

|  | N | Mean | SD | SE |
|---|---|---|---|---|
| **Democrat State** | 36 | 10.877 | 1.843 | .3072 |
| **Republican State** | 42 | 10.483 | 1.833 | .2829 |

++++++++++++++++++++++++++++++++++++++++++++++++++++++++


**Partisan State and Males Being Cyberbullied**

Levene's test is not significant; therefore, equal variances are assumed.

**Dependent Variable: Cyberbullied Males**

+++++++++++++++++++++++++++++++++++++++++++++++++++++++++++

| | Levene's test for Equality of Variance | | | | Sig. |
|---|---|---|---|---|---|
| | F | Sig | t | df | (2-tailed) |

+++++++++++++++++++++++++++++++++++++++++++++++++++++++++++

| **Equal Variances Assumed** | .025 | .875 | .945 | 76 | .348 |
| Equal variances not Assumed | | | .944 | 74.068 | .348 |

+++++++++++++++++++++++++++++++++++++++++++++++++++++++++++

# Summary of Democrat states (1) and Republican states(2)

M1 = 10.877, SD1 = 1.843, SE1 = .3072

M2 = 10.483, SD2 = 1.833, SE2 = .2829

$t$ (76) = .945, p ≥ .05, two-tailed

There was no significant difference in male students who were electronically bullied between Democrat states and Republican states. Although not statistically significant, the male students who were electronically bullied in Republican states (M2 = 10.483, SD2 = 1.833, SE2 = .2829) had a slightly lower mean than male students in Democrat states

(M1 = 10.877, SD1 = 1.843, SE1 = .3072), p ≥ .05, two-tailed.

## Independent Samples t-test – Partisanship and Total Students

An independent samples t-test was performed to compare total students who were electronically bullied in Democrat (1) states and in Republican (2) states. See Table 4. The Levene's test is not significant; therefore, equal variances are assumed. Because the researcher is uncertain which political party, if any, will influence electronic bullying, a two-tailed test has been employed.

Table 4
*T-test Results: Partisanship and Total Percent Students*

**Dependent Variable: Total Students Being Cyberbullied**

+++++++++++++++++++++++++++++++++++++++++++++++++++++++++++++++

|  | N | Mean | SD | SE |
|---|---|---|---|---|
| **Democrat State** | 36 | 15.688 | 2.496 | .4161 |
| **Republican State** | 42 | 16.421 | 2.229 | .3440 |

+++++++++++++++++++++++++++++++++++++++++++++++++++++++++++++++

**Partisan State and Total Students Being Cyberbullied**

Levene's test is not significant; therefore, equal variances are assumed.

**Dependent Variable: Cyberbullied Total Students**

+++++++++++++++++++++++++++++++++++++++++++++++++++++++++++++++

|  | Levene's test for Equality of Variance | | | | Sig. |
|---|---|---|---|---|---|
|  | F | Sig | t | df | (2-tailed) |
| **Equal Variances Assumed** | .329 | .568 | -1.369 | 76 | .175 |
| Equal variances not Assumed |  |  | -1.357 | 70.917 | .179 |

+++++++++++++++++++++++++++++++++++++++++++++++++++++++++++++++

## Summary of Democrat states (1) and Republican states (2)

M1 = 15.688, SD1 = 2.496, SE1 = .4161

M2 = 16.421, SD2 = 2.229, SE2 = .3440

$t$ (76) = -1.369, p ≥ .05, two-tailed

There was no significant difference in the total students who were electronically bullied between Democrat states and Republican states. Although not statistically significant, the total students who were electronically bullied in Republican states (M2 = 16.421, SD2 = 2.229, SE2 = .3440) had a higher mean than in Democrat states (M1 = 15.688, SD1 = 2.496, SE1 = .4161); p ≥ .05, two-tailed.

**Figure 14. Significance of cyberbullying and having suicidal thoughts.**

## The Percentage of Female Students Who were Electronically Bullied (EBF) and the Percentage of Female Students Who Seriously Considered Attempting Suicide (SF)

A simple linear regression was used to determine the relationship between female students who were cyberbullied and female students who had suicidal thoughts. The results were as follows: $F_{(1,76)} = 7.207$, $p = .009$ (significant). The null hypothesis is rejected; thus, there is a statistically significant relationship between the percentage of female students who were electronically bullied (EBF) and the percentage of female students who seriously considered attempting suicide (SF). The regression equation used to predict SF based on EBF was determined as follows: SF = 15.159 + .211 (EBF), $R^2 = .087$.

## The Percentage of Male Students Who were Electronically Bullied (EBM) and the Percentage of Male Students Who Seriously Considered Attempting Suicide (SM)

A simple linear regression was used to determine the relationship between male students who were cyberbullied and male students who had suicidal thoughts. The results were as follows: $F_{(1,76)} = 9.092$, $p = .003$ (significant). The null hypothesis is rejected; thus, there is a statistically significant relationship between the percentage of male students who were electronically bullied (EBM) and the percentage of male students who seriously considered attempting suicide (SM). The regression equation used to predict SM based on EBM was determined as follows: SM = 8.394 + .299 (EBM), $R^2 = .107$.

## The Total Percentage of Students Who were Electronically Bullied (EBT) and the Total Percentage of Students Who Seriously Considered Attempting Suicide (ST)

A simple linear regression was used to determine the relationship between total students who were cyberbullied and total students who had suicidal thoughts. The results were as follows: $F_{(1,76)} = 5.709$, $p = .019$ (significant). The null hypothesis is rejected; thus, there is a statistically significant relationship between the total percentage of students who were electronically bullied (EBT) and the total percentage of students who seriously considered attempting suicide (ST). The regression equation used to predict ST based on EBT was determined as follows: ST = 12.272 + .209 (EBT), $R^2 = .070$.

## R-squared (R2)

R-squared (R2) is a statistical measure (explained variation / total variation) of how close the data are to the fitted regression line (Frost, 2013). R2 always lies between 0% and 100%. The higher the R2, the better the model explains all the variability of the response data around the mean. In the current study, the models only explained 7.0% to 10.7% of the outcome. In other words, variables not considered in the study accounted for most of the explained outcome (Allison, 1999). Thus, the present study's model is not a good fit for the data and it explains very little of the variability of the response data around the mean.

However, R2 may be low in the social science field because human emotions are harder to predict than physical processes (Frost, 2013). Although the R2 values were small, this does not necessarily mean that the models should be rejected (Allison, 1999). Indeed, there are still statistically significant relationships between the variables. In other words, the independent variables can still predict the dependent variables. Furthermore, although a high R2 is desirable, it is not sufficient by itself (Frost, 2013).

## Power Analysis

The sample size for the current study was 78, with 36 being Democrat states and 42 being Republican states. To determine the minimum sample size needed to detect a significant effect for this study, a priori power analysis based on two-sample t-test was conducted using Gpower 3.1.9.2 (Faul, Erdfelder, Buchner, & Lang, 2009; Su, 2017). Assuming a large effect size (Cohen's d = 0.8) and a significance level of 0.05, the minimum sample size required for the study to detect a significant effect with 80% power is 52 (Cohen, 1988; Peng & Davis, 2017b; Su, 2017).

# Conclusion

This chapter presented the statistical analyses and findings of the current study. The results of the independent samples t-tests indicate that female students in Democrat states are less likely to be cyberbullied than in Republican states. However, there was no significant difference for male students.

The results of the linear regression analyses indicate that students who are cyberbullied will seriously consider suicide. The results were significant for both males and females. Thus, once students are cyberbullied, they will seriously consider suicide. A further discussion of the findings is presented in Chapter 5. Chapter 5 also describes the practical implications, limitations, and recommendations for future research.

# CHAPTER 5

## Summary of the Results

This study used independent samples t-tests and linear regression analyses on secondary data to answer the research questions. The findings of the t-tests indicate that a) there is a statistically significant difference between partisanship and the percentage of female students who were electronically bullied, b) there is no statistically significant difference between partisanship and the percentage of male students who were electronically bullied, and c) there is no statistically significant difference between partisanship and the total percentage of students who were electronically bullied. In addition, linear regression analyses indicate that there are statistically significant relationships between being cyberbullied and having suicidal thoughts, for both male students and female students, although the R-squared values are low.

## Discussion of Results

The purpose of the current study was to answer the following two general research questions. Is there a difference between Democrat and Republican states and the percentage of students who were electronically bullied? Is there a relationship between the percentage of students who were cyberbullied and the percentage of students who seriously considered attempting suicide? For each of the two general research questions, females and males were assessed separately and then jointly as a total group. In order to answer the research questions, SPSS was used to assess the data.

The findings suggest that there is a difference between partisanship and the percentage of female students who were electronically bullied. Females students who were in Republican states were cyberbullied more often. However, there is no statistically significant difference for male students or for total students. In addition, the findings indicate that there is a relationship between students who were electronically bullied and students who seriously considered attempting suicide. The relationship exists for female students, male students, and total students. In short, once students were electronically bullied, they seriously considered suicide.

# Discussion of the Conclusions

The deterrence theory as implemented by the Democrats seems to better protect female students against cyberbullying, which may promote public safety. The results of the independent samples t-tests indicate that female students in Democrat states were less likely to be cyberbullied than female students in Republican states; however, there is no statistically significance difference between partisanship and the percentage of male students who were cyberbullied. The results of linear regression analyses indicate that once female students and male students were cyberbullied, they seriously considered attempting suicide. Therefore, the problem of suicidal thoughts may be addressed through appropriate laws that control cyberbullying, which can be enforced by a political party via the deterrence theory.

# Practical Implications

This study is useful because it suggests that political parties can influence cyberbullying and the percentage of students who seriously consider attempting suicide. The Democrat party and the Republican party have different paradigms on laws and government interventions (Deffen, n.d.; Kenneth, 2012; Kneeland, 2016). Both parties have the authority to pass laws that deter crime, such as cyberbullying. Thus, because the Democrat states have a lower rate of cyberbullying than do the Republican states, this study may provide valuable insight into laws that reduce cyberbullying and reduce suicidal thoughts. The findings of this study add value to the body of knowledge in better understanding cyberbullying and suicidal thoughts. Indeed, this study indicates the need for additional research.

# Limitations

There are several limitations in this study, which may impact the results and conclusions. First, because the study has a correlational design, it does not reflect causal relationships (Bordens & Abbott, 2008). Second, because the sample is restricted to school students in grades 9-12 in the United States, the findings cannot be generalized to other populations (Eaton et al., 2012; Kann et al., 2014; Kann et al., 2016). Third, because the data indicate crime rates, and many crimes are not reported by victims, the data may be incomplete (Centers for Disease Control and Prevention, 2014). Fourth, because cyberbullying is a recent problem, there are only 3 years of data available (2011, 2013, and 2015). Thus, the amount of data available is less than optimal. Fifth, because the data used in the study are second-hand and collected for a different reason, the data values cannot be more clearly defined (Denscombe, 2007). Finally, because the study is quantitative in nature, it does not provide the reasons why people behave in certain manners (Berg, 2007).

# Recommendations for Future Research

The current study investigated a) the difference between partisanship and the percentage of students who were electronically bullied, and b) the relationship between the percentage of students who were electronically bullied and the percentage of students who seriously considered attempting suicide. Considering the assumptions and limitations in the study, there are some recommendations for future research.

First, one limitation in the current study is that electronic government-based secondary data were used. The data were collected for a certain purpose, which may not completely meet the objectives of the current study (Denscombe, 2007). Therefore, a future study may collect primary data via a survey that is in better alignment with the study's theory. Second, the participants in the current study consisted of high school students in grades 9-12 in the United States. Instead of examining high school students, future studies may investigate different age groups, such as primary school students and adults. Third, the current study defined each state as either Republican or Democrat by how the state voted in prior Presidential elections. Thus, future research may categorize party affiliation in a different manner. For example, the states may be categorized by their House of Representatives and Senate partisanship.

**Figure 15. Land of the free to be free from harm.**

# APPENDIX

## Select SPSS Data Results

Linear regression is a parametric statistic and is useful for determining the relationships between continuous variables. For linear regression, the model assumptions are 1) independence (independent observations), 2) normality (residuals are normally distributed), 3) homoscedasticity (residuals have constant variance), and 4) linearity (linear relationship between the independent and dependent variables) (Norusis, 2012; Su, 2017). Following are select SPSS results that check the model's assumptions.

## Checking the Normality of Data

### Stem & Leaf

## The total percentage of students who were electronically bullied (EBT) Score Frequency

| Frequency | Stem & Leaf |
|---|---|
| 2.00 | 1 . 11 |
| 16.00 | 1 . 2222233333333333 |
| 23.00 | 1 . 44444444455555555555555 |
| 17.00 | 1 . 66666677777777777 |
| 16.00 | 1 . 8888888888888999 |
| 4.00 | 2 . 0011 |

Stem width: 10.00

Each leaf: 1 case(s)

# Checking the Normality of Data

## Stem & Leaf

## The total percentage of students who seriously considered attempting suicide (ST) Score Frequency

| Frequency | Stem & Leaf |
|-----------|-------------|
| 1.00 | 11 . 4 |
| 4.00 | 12 . 1139 |
| 8.00 | 13 . 02347899 |
| 16.00 | 14 . 0123333455667778 |
| 16.00 | 15 . 0222344567777899 |
| 18.00 | 16 . 00000111222577899 |
| 6.00 | 17 . 033458 |
| 5.00 | 18 . 17899 |
| 2.00 | 19 . 08 |
| 1.00 | 20 . 1 |
| 1.00 Extremes | (>=20.3) |

Stem width:      1.00

Each leaf:      1 case(s)

# Checking the Normality of Data

## Histogram of the total percentage of students who were electronically bullied (EBT)

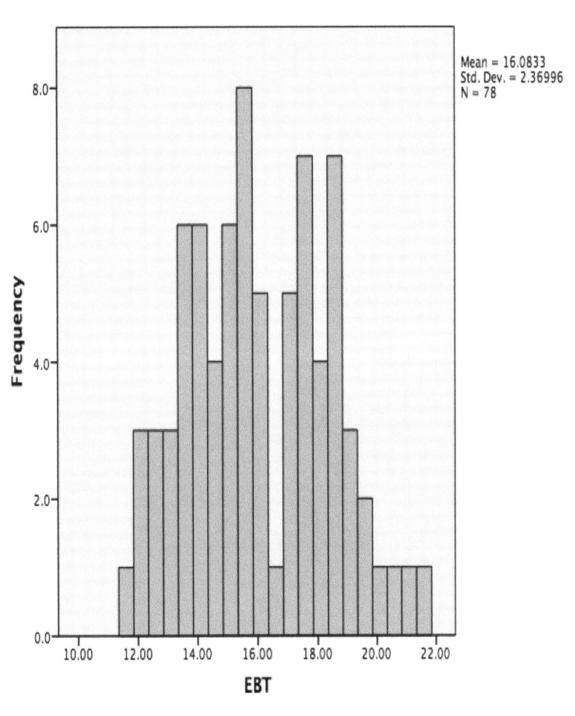

# Checking the Normality of Data

## Histogram of the total percentage of students who seriously considered attempting suicide (ST)

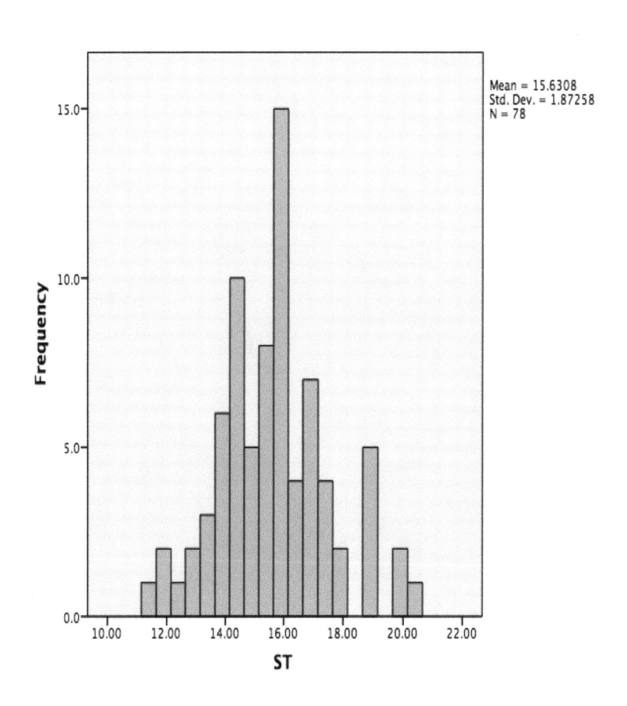

# Checking the Normality of Data

## Boxplot of the total percentage of students who were electronically bullied (EBT)

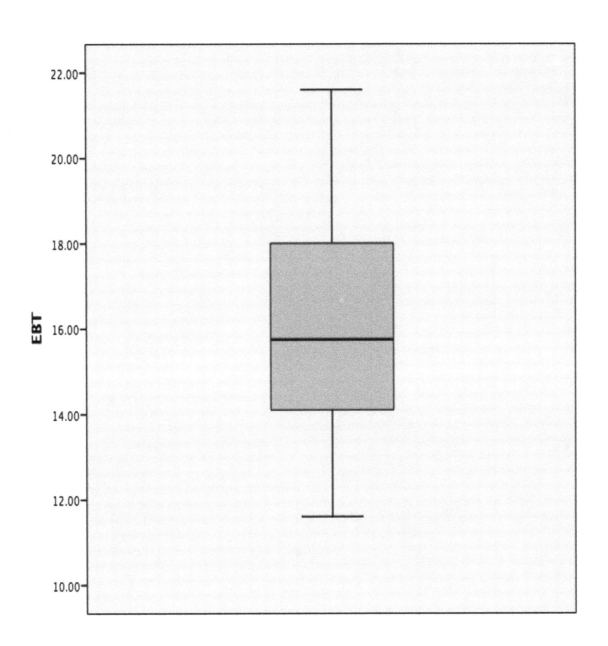

# Checking the Normality of Data

## Histogram of the total percentage of students who seriously considered attempting suicide (ST)

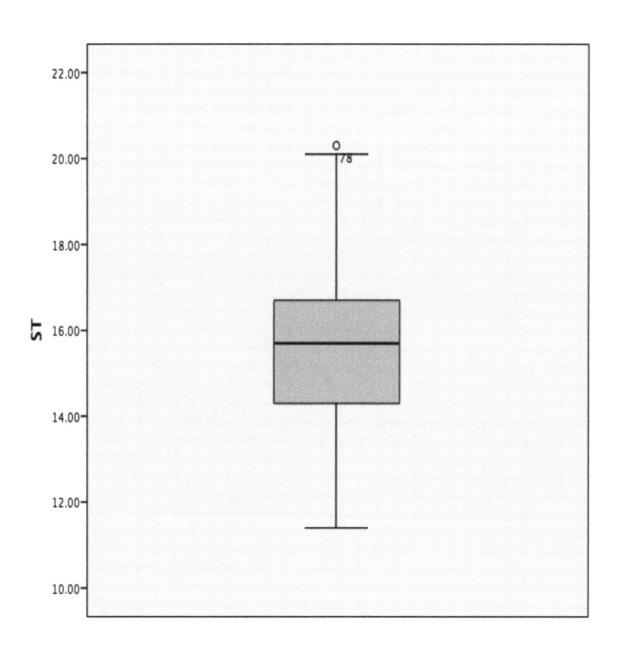

# Checking the Normality of Data

## Q-Q Plot of the total percentage of students who were electronically bullied (EBT)

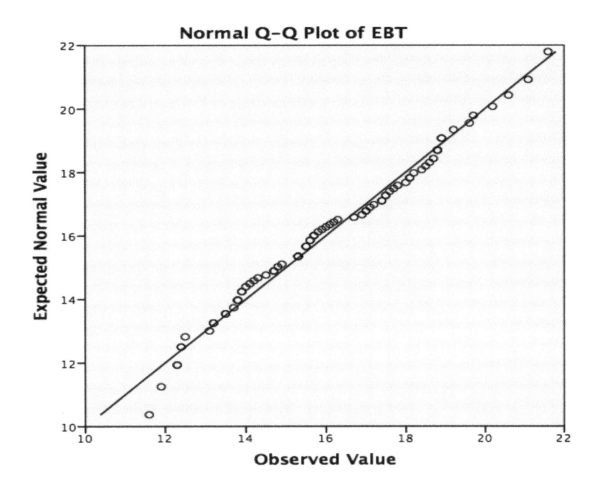

The normal probability plot, or Q-Q plot, is used to determine if the data appear to come from a normal distribution (Norusis, 2012). Because most of the EBT data cluster around a straight line, this indicates that the distribution of the EBT data is close to normal.

# Checking the Normality of Data

## Q-Q Plot of the total percentage of students who seriously considered attempting suicide (ST)

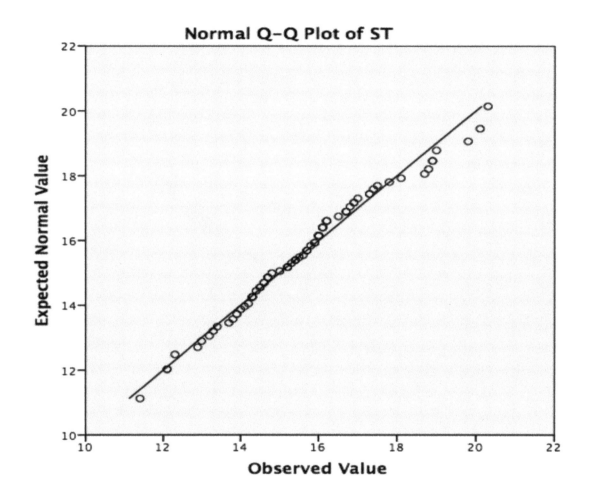

The normal probability plot, or Q-Q plot, is used to determine if the data appear to come from a normal distribution (Norusis, 2012). Because most of the ST data cluster around a straight line, this indicates that the distribution of the ST data is close to normal.

# Checking Residuals

When using linear regression, residuals are used to detect departures from the regression assumptions. If the assumptions for regression are satisfied, then the residuals should have the following four characteristics: 1) the residuals should be approximately normally distributed, 2) successive residuals should be approximately independent, 3) the variance for the dependent variable should be the same for all values of the independent variable, and 4) the residuals should show no pattern when plotted against the predicted values (Norusis, 2008).

## Checking if residuals are approximately normally distributed

The Q-Q plot of Studentized residual is used to check if the residuals are approximately normally distributed. Because most of the data cluster around a straight line, this indicates that the distribution of the residuals is close to normal.

## Q-Q Plot of Studentized Residuals

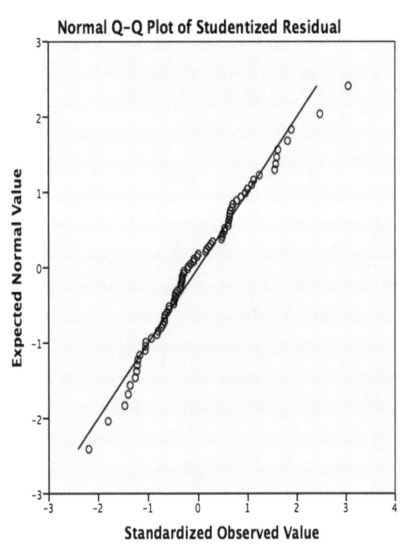

# Checking for Constant Variance

To check the constant variance assumption, the variance for the dependent variable should be the same for all values of the independent variable. This can be visually checked by looking at the plot of the Studentized residuals against the predicted values. If there is constant variance, then the plot should not show a pattern. The residuals should appear randomly scattered around a horizontal line through zero. Because the residuals do appear randomly scattered around a horizontal line through zero, the constant variance assumption has been satisfied. This was true for all three plots: a) the percentage of female students who were electronically bullied and the percentage of female students who seriously considered attempting suicide, b) the percentage of male students who were electronically bullied and the percentage of male students who seriously considered attempting suicide, and c) the total percentage of students who were electronically bullied and the total percentage of students who seriously considered attempting suicide.

## Checking for Constant Variance Plot 1

## Studentized Residuals versus Predicted Values Scatterplot

## The percentage of female students who were electronically bullied (EBF)

## and the percentage of female students who seriously considered

## attempting suicide (SF), Regression

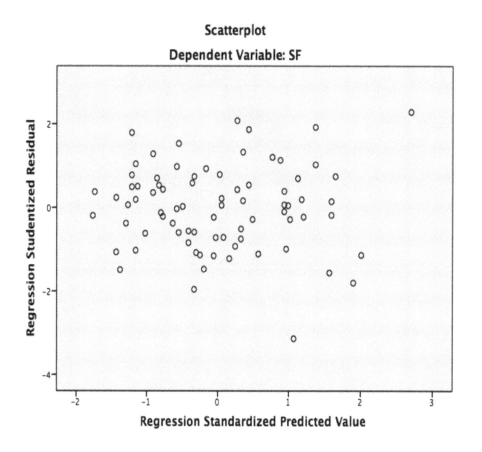

# Checking for Constant Variance Plot 2

## The percentage of male students who were electronically bullied (EBM) and the percentage of male students who seriously considered attempting suicide (SM), Regression

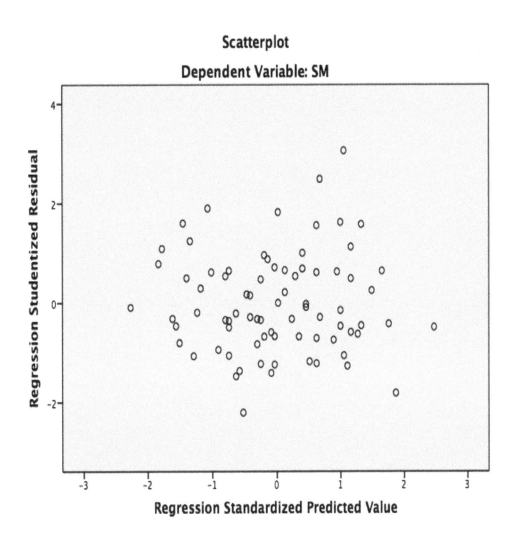

# Checking for Constant Variance Plot 3

## The total percentage of students who were electronically bullied (EBT) and the total percentage of students who seriously considered attempting suicide (ST), Regression

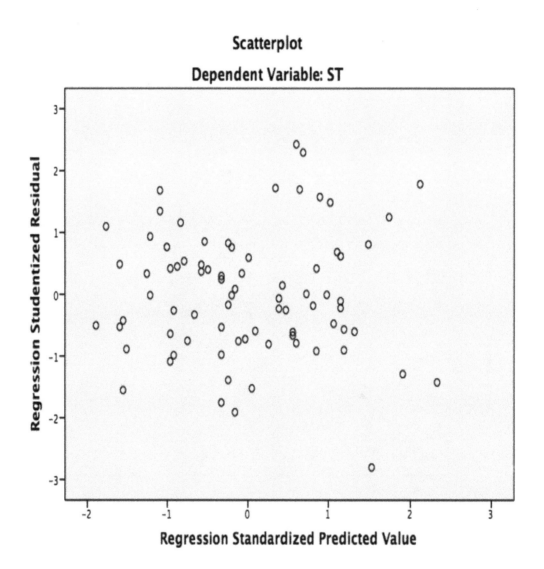

Scatterplot

Dependent Variable: ST

# Checking Linear Regression Independent Observations

For linear regression, there is an independent observation assumption (Field, 2005). The Durbin-Watson statistic is useful for determining if adjacent residuals are correlated and if the independent errors assumption is satisfied (Field, 2005). The Durbin-Watson statistic can vary from 0 to 4. A Durbin-Watson value of 2 means that the residuals are independent.

For the current study, the independent errors assumption was checked using the Durbin-Watson statistic, which was 1.589 for females, 1.780 for males, and 1.625 for the total group. A value of the Durbin-Watson statistic between 1.5 and 2.5 suggests that the independence assumption holds true (Norusis, 2012; Su, 2017). Thus, the regression model's independent errors assumption appears to have been satisfied.

## Durbin-Watson Test 1

### Model Summary[b] (Females)

| Model | R | R Square | Adjusted R Square | Std. Error of the Estimate | Durbin-Watson |
|---|---|---|---|---|---|
| 1 | .294[a] | .087 | .075 | 2.50444 | 1.589 |

a. Predictors: (Constant), EBF

b. Dependent Variable: SF

# Durbin-Watson Test 2

### Model Summary[b] (Males)

| Model | R | R Square | Adjusted R Square | Std. Error of the Estimate | Durbin-Watson |
|---|---|---|---|---|---|
| 1 | .327[a] | .107 | .095 | 1.59985 | 1.780 |

a. Predictors: (Constant), EBM

b. Dependent Variable: SM

# Durbin-Watson Test 3

### Model Summary[b] (Total)

| Model | R | R Square | Adjusted R Square | Std. Error of the Estimate | Durbin-Watson |
|---|---|---|---|---|---|
| 1 | .294[a] | .070 | .058 | 1.81782 | 1.625 |

a. Predictors: (Constant), EBT

b. Dependent Variable: ST

# Regression Analysis 1

## The percentage of female students who were electronically bullied (EBF) and the percentage of female students who seriously considered attempting suicide (SF)

**Model Summary**

| Model | R | R Square | Adjusted R Square | Std. Error of the Estimate |
|-------|-----|----------|-------------------|----------------------------|
| 1 | .294[a] | .087 | .075 | 2.50444 |

a. Predictors: (Constant), EBF

**ANOVA[a]**

| Model | | Sum of Squares | df | Mean Square | F | Sig. |
|-------|------------|---------------|----|-------------|-------|-------|
| 1 | Regression | 45.203 | 1 | 45.203 | 7.207 | .009[b] |
| | Residual | 476.690 | 76 | 6.272 | | |
| | Total | 521.893 | 77 | | | |

a. Dependent Variable: SF

b. Predictors: (Constant), EBF

| Model | Unstandardized Coefficients | | Standardized Coefficients | t | Sig. |
|---|---|---|---|---|---|
| | B | Std. Error | Beta | | |
| 1 (Constant) | 15.159 | 1.723 | | 8.797 | .000 |
| EBF | .211 | .079 | .294 | 2.685 | .009 |

**Summary of EBF and SF**

$F(1,76) = 7.207$, $p = .009$ (significant)

$SF = 15.159 + .211$ (EBF), $R2 = .087$

There is a statistically significant relationship between the percentage of female students who were electronically bullied (EBF) and the percentage of female students who seriously considered attempting suicide (SF).

# Regression Analysis 2

## The percentage of male students who were electronically bullied (EBM) and the percentage of male students who seriously considered attempting suicide (SM)

**Model Summary**

| Model | R | R Square | Adjusted R Square | Std. Error of the Estimate |
|-------|------|----------|-------------------|----------------------------|
| 1 | .327[a] | .107 | .095 | 1.59985 |

a. Predictors: (Constant), EBM

**ANOVA[a]**

| Model | | Sum of Squares | df | Mean Square | F | Sig. |
|-------|------------|----------------|----|-------------|-------|--------|
| 1 | Regression | 23.270 | 1 | 23.270 | 9.092 | .003[b] |
| | Residual | 194.524 | 76 | 2.560 | | |
| | Total | 217.794 | 77 | | | |

a. Dependent Variable: SM

b. Predictors: (Constant), EBM

| Model | Unstandardized Coefficients | | Standardized Coefficients | t | Sig. |
|---|---|---|---|---|---|
| | B | Std. Error | Beta | | |
| 1 (Constant) | 8.394 | 1.074 | | 7.817 | .000 |
| EBM | .299 | .099 | .327 | 3.015 | .003 |

## Summary of EBM and SM

$F$ (1,76) = 9.092, p = .003 (significant)

SM = 8.394 + .299 (EBM), R2 = .107

There is a statistically significant relationship between the percentage of male students who were electronically bullied (EBM) and the percentage of male students who seriously considered attempting suicide (SM).

# Regression Analysis 3

## The total percentage of students who were electronically bullied (EBT) and the total percentage of students who seriously considered attempting suicide (ST)

**Model Summary**

| Mode 1 | R | R Square | Adjusted R Square | Std. Error of the Estimate |
|---|---|---|---|---|
| 1 | .264[a] | .070 | .058 | 1.81782 |

a. Predictors: (Constant), EBT

**ANOVA[a]**

| | Model | Sum of Squares | df | Mean Square | F | Sig. |
|---|---|---|---|---|---|---|
| 1 | Regression | 18.866 | 1 | 18.866 | 5.709 | .019[b] |
| | Residual | 251.140 | 76 | 3.304 | | |
| | Total | 270.006 | 77 | | | |

a. Dependent Variable: ST

b. Predictors: (Constant), EBT

| Model | Unstandardized Coefficients | | Standardized Coefficients | t | Sig. |
|---|---|---|---|---|---|
| | B | Std. Error | Beta | | |
| 1 (Constant) | 12.272 | 1.421 | | 8.637 | .000 |
| EBT | .209 | .087 | .264 | 2.389 | .019 |

## Summary of EBT and ST

$F(1,76) = 5.709$, $p = .019$ (significant)

$ST = 12.272 + .209 (EBT)$, $R2 = .070$

There is a statistically significant relationship between the total percentage of students who were electronically bullied (EBT) and the total percentage of students who seriously considered attempting suicide (ST).

## Independent Samples *t*-Test

## Democrat and Republican states and the percentage of female students who were electronically bullied (EBF)

## Group Statistics

| Democrat = 1<br><br>Republican = 2 | N | Mean | Std.<br><br>Deviation | Std. Error<br><br>Mean |
|---|---|---|---|---|
| 1 | 36 | 20.5278 | 3.58286 | .59714 |
| 2 | 42 | 22.5476 | 3.44293 | .53126 |

| | Levene's Test for Equality of Variances | | t-test for Equality of Means | | | | | | |
|---|---|---|---|---|---|---|---|---|---|
| | | | | | | | | 95% Confidence | |
| | F | Sig. | t | df | Sig. (2-tailed) | Mean Diff | Std. Error Diff. | Lower | Upper |
| Equal variances assumed | .135 | .714 | -2.535 | 76 | .013 | -2.0198 | .79678 | -3.6067 | -.4329 |
| Equal variances not assumed | | | -2.527 | 73.19 | .014 | -2.0198 | .79926 | -3.6126 | -.4269 |

**Summary of Democrat state (1) and Republican state (2)**

M1 = 20.527, SD1 = 3.582, SE1 = .5971

M2 = 22.547, SD2 = 3.442, SE2 = .5312

$t$ (76) = -2.535, p ≤ .05, two-tailed

There is a significant difference between Democrat and Republican states and the percentage of female students who were electronically bullied (EBF).

## Democrat and Republican states and the total percentage of male students who were electronically bullied (EBM)

### Group Statistics

| Democrat = 1<br>Republican = 2 | N | Mean | Std.<br>Deviation | Std. Error<br>Mean |
|---|---|---|---|---|
| 1 | 36 | 10.8778 | 1.84346 | .30724 |
| 2 | 42 | 10.4833 | 1.83395 | .28298 |

| | Levene's Test for Equality of Variances | | t-test for Equality of Means | | | | | | |
| --- | --- | --- | --- | --- | --- | --- | --- | --- | --- |
| | | | | | | | | 95% Confidence | |
| | F | Sig. | t | df | Sig. (2-tailed) | Mean Diff | Std. Error Diff. | Lower | Upper |
| Equal variances assumed | .025 | .875 | .945 | 76 | .348 | .3944 | .4175 | -.4371 | 1.2260 |
| Equal variances not assumed | | | .944 | 74.06 | .348 | .3944 | .4177 | -.4378 | 1.2267 |

## Summary of Democrat state (1) and Republican state (2)

M1 = 10.877, SD1 = 1.843, SE1 = .3072

M2 = 10.483, SD2 = 1.833, SE2 = .2829

$t$ (76) = .945, p ≥ .05, two-tailed

There is no significant difference between Democrat and Republican states and the percentage of male students who were electronically bullied (EBM).

# Democrat and Republican states and the total percentage of students who were electronically bullied (EBT)

## Group Statistics

| Democrat = 1<br>Republican = 2 | N | Mean | Std.<br>Deviation | Std. Error<br>Mean |
|---|---|---|---|---|
| 1 | 36 | 15.6889 | 2.49694 | .41616 |
| 2 | 42 | 16.4214 | 2.22990 | .34408 |

| | Levene's Test for Equality of Variances | | t-test for Equality of Means | | | | | | |
|---|---|---|---|---|---|---|---|---|---|
| | | | | | | | | 95%<br>Confidence | |
| | F | Sig. | t | df | Sig.<br>(2-tailed) | Mean<br>Diff | Std.<br>Error<br>Diff. | Lower | Upper |
| Equal variances assumed | .329 | .568 | -1.369 | 76 | .175 | -.7325 | .5352 | -1.7986 | .3335 |
| Equal variances not assumed | | | -1.357 | 70.91 | .179 | -.7325 | .5399 | -1.8092 | .3441 |

**Summary of Democrat state (1) and Republican state (2)**

M1 = 15.688, SD1 = 2.496, SE1 = .4161

M2 = 16.421, SD2 = 2.229, SE2 = .3440

$t$ (76) = -1.369, p ≥ .05, two-tailed

There is no significant difference between Democrat and Republican states and the total percentage of students who were electronically bullied (EBT).

**Figure 16. Take the bull by the horns and stop electronic bullying**

# REFERENCES

Akers, R. L., & Sellers, C. S. (2009). *Criminological Theories*. NY: Oxford University Press.

Allison, P.D. (1999). *Multiple regression*: A primer. Thousand Oaks, CA: Pine Forge.

Allison, M. S., & William, J. F. (2012). Prevalence, psychological impact, and coping of cyberbully victims among college students. *Journal of School Violence*, 11(1), 21-37.

Berg, B. L. (2007). *Qualitative research methods for the social sciences* (6th ed). Boston, MA: Pearson Education, Inc.

Bordens, K., & Abbott, B. (2008). Research design and methods: A process approach (7th ed.). Boston, MA: McGraw Hill.

Brener, N. D., Kann, L., McManus, T., Kinchen, S.A., Sundberg, E. C., & Ross, J. G. (2002). Reliability of the 1999 Youth Risk Behavior Survey questionnaire. Journal of Adolescent Health, 31(4), 336-342.

Brownfield, D. & Sorenson, A. (1993). Self-control and juvenile delinquency: Theoretical issues and an empirical assessment of selected elements of a general theory of crime. Deviant Behavior, 14, 243-264.

Carney, J. V. (2000). Bullied to death. School Psychology International, 21(2), 213-223.

Centers for Disease Control and Prevention. (2014). Morbidity and Morality Weekly Report. Retrieved from http://www.cdc.gov/mmwr/pdf/ss/ss6304.pdf

Champion, D. (2006). Research methods for criminal justice and criminology

(3rd ed.).  Upper Saddle River, NJ: Pearson Merrill Prentice Hall.

Chiricos T. G., & Waldo G. P. (1970).  Punishment and crime: An examination of some empirical evidence. *Social Problems, 18*, 200-217.

Cohen, J. (1988). *Statistical power analysis for the behavior science.* Lawrance Eribaum Association.

Davis W. L. (2015). *Police-community relations: Bridging the gap.* Bloomington, IN: Xlibris.

Deffen (n.d.). *Democrat versus Republican.* Retrieved from http://www. diffen.com/difference/Democrat_vs_Republican

Denscombe, M. (2007). *The good research guide: for small-scale social research projects* (4th ed.).  Open University Press.

Eaton, D.K., Kann, L., Kinchen, S., Shanklin, S., Flint, K.H., Hawkins, J., Harris, W.A., Lowry, R., McManus, T., Chyen, D. & Whittle, L. (2012). Youth risk behavior surveillance—United States, 2011. *Morbidity and Mortality Weekly Report: Surveillance Summaries*, 61(4), 1-162.  Retrieved from  https://www.cdc.gov/mmwr/pdf/ss/ss6104.pdf

Faul, F., Erdfelder, E., Buchner, A., & Lang, A. G. (2009). Statistical power analyses using G* Power 3.1: Tests for correlation and regression analyses. *Behavior Research Methods, 41*(4), 1149-1160.

Field, A. (2005). *Discovering statistics using SPSS* (2nd ed.). Thousand Oaks, CA: Sage Publications.

Frost J. (2013). *Regression analysis: How do I interpret R-squared and assess the goodness-of-fit?* Retrieved from http://blog.minitab.com/blog/ adventures-in-statistics-2/regression-analysis-how-do-i-interpret-r-squared-and-assess-the-goodness-of-fit

Gibbs J. P. (1968). Crime, punishment, and deterrence. *Southwestern Social Science Quarterly, 48*, 515-530.

Hertz M. F., Donato I., & Wright J. (2013). *Bullying and suicide: a public health approach.* Retrieved from http://www.ncdsv.org/images/JAH_Bullying-and-Suicide-a-public-health-approach_7-2013.pdf

Hinduja S. & Patchin J. W. (2010). *International academy for suicide research: Bullying, cyberbullying, and suicide.* doi: 10.1080/13811118.2010.494133

Hinduja S. & Patchin J. W. (2015). *Cyberbullying legislation and case law-implications for school policy and practice.* Retrieved from http://cyberbullying.org/cyberbullying-legal-issues.pdf

Hinduja S. & Patchin J. W. (2016). *State cyberbullying laws: A brief review of state cyberbullying laws and policies.* Retrieved from http://cyberbullying.org/Bullying-and-Cyberbullying-Laws.pdf

Kann, L., Kinchen, S., Shanklin, S.L., Flint, K.H., Hawkins, J., Harris, W.A., Lowry, R., Olsen, E.O.M., McManus, T., Chyen, D., Whittle, L., Taylor, E., Demissie, Z., Brener, N., Thornton, J., Moore, J., & Zaza, S. (2014). Youth risk behavior surveillance—United States, 2013. *MMWR. Surveillance Summaries*, 64. Retrieved from https://www.cdc.gov/mmwr/pdf/ss/ss6304.pdf

Kann, L., McManus, T., Harris, W.A., Shanklin, S.L., Flint, K.H., Hawkins, J., Queen, B., Lowry, R., Olsen, E., Chyen, D., Whittle, L., Thornton, J., Lim, C., Yamakawa, Y., Brener, N., & Zaza, S. (2016). Youth risk behavior surveillance—United States, 2015. *MMWR. Surveillance Summaries*, 65. Retrieved from https://www.cdc.gov/healthyyouth/data/yrbs/pdf/2015/ss6506_updated.pdf

Kenneth C. (2012). *Tech policy 2012: Comparing the Democrat's and Republican's platforms.* Retrieved from http://www.cio.com/article/2392434/government/tech-policy-2012--comparing-the-democrat-s-and-republican-s-platforms.html

Kim Y. S., Koh Y., & Leventhal B. (2005). School bullying and suicidal risk in Korean middle school students. *Pediatrics, 15*, 357-363.

Kneeland T. W. (2016). *Today's social issues: Democrats and Republicans: Democrats and Republicans.* Retrieved from https:// books.google.com/books?

id=8vlUDAAAQBAJ&pg=PA49&lpg=PA49&dq=republican+and +democrat+cyberbullying&source=bl&ots=wRRelf8d9R&sig=i4f WQdUM8nHMaemXK7iuC5h34C8&hl=en&sa=X&ved=0ahUKEwjY_ Zee9brRAhUp2oMKHYj5BKkQ6AEIVjAM#v=onepage&q =republican%20and%20democrat%20cyberbullying&f=false

Kowalski R. M., Limber, S.P., & Agatston, P.W. (2012). *Cyberbullying: Bullying in the digital age.* Wiley-Blackwell.

Kraut, R., Mukhopadhyay, T., Szczypula, J., Kiesler, S., & Scherlis, W. (1998). Communication and information: Alternative uses of the Internet in households. *CHI '98 Proceedings of the SIGCHI Conference on Human Factors in Computing Systems*, 368-375. doi: 10.1145/274644.274695

Lebo H. (2010). *Surveying the digital future.* Retrieved from http://www. digitalcenter.org/wp-content/uploads/2012/12/2010_digital_future_report-year9.pdf

Leedy P., & Ormrod J. (2005). *Practical Research: Planning and design* (8th ed). Upper Saddle River, NJ: Pearson Merrill Prentice Hall.

Long, J.S. (1997). *Regression models for categorical and limited dependent variables.* Sage Publishing.

Lunenburg F. C., & Irby B. J. (2007). *Writing a successful thesis or dissertation: Tips and strategies for students in the social and behavioral sciences. Location: Corwin Press.*

Mitchell, S.L., Kiely, D.K., Miller, S.C., Connor, S.R., Spence, C., & Teno, J.M. (2007). Hospice care for patients with dementia. *Journal of Pain and Symptom Management, 34*(1), 7-16.

Nagin D. S., & Pogarsky G. (2001). Integrating celerity, impulsivity, and extralegal sanction threats into a model of general deterrence: Theory and evidence. *Criminology, 39*, 865-892.

Norusis M. J. (2008). *Statistics 16.0 guide to data analysis.* Upper Saddle, River, NJ: Prentice Hall.

Norusis M. J. (2012). Statistics 19 guide to data analysis. Upper Saddle, River, NJ: Prentice Hall.

Ostermeier E. (2009). *Red states had higher crimes rates than blue states.* Retrieved from http://editions.lib.umn.edu/smartpolitics/2009/09/16/red-states-have-higher-crime-r/

Patchin J. W., & Hinduja S. (2013). *Cyberbullying among Adolescents: Implications for Empirical Research.* Retrieved from http://www.jahonline. org/article/S1054-139X(13)00412-6/pdf

Peng, Y, & Davis, W.L. (2017a). Cyberbullying & Suicidal Thoughts in the United States. *Asian Academic Research Journal of Social Sciences and Humanities, 4*(7), 102-109.

Peng, Y, & Davis, W.L. (2017b). Partisanship and Cyberbullying in the

United States. *Asian Academic Research Journal of Social Sciences and Humanities, 4*(7), 133-139.

Perren, S., Dooley, J., Shaw, T., & Cross, D. (2010). Bullying in school and cyberspace: Associations with depressive symptoms in Swiss and Australian adolescents. *Child and Adolescent Psychiatry and Mental Health.* doi:10.1186/1753-2000-4-28.

Poe, C. (Executive Producer) & Poe, C. & Parker, G. (Writers). (2006). World's most dangerous gang [Motion Picture]. United States: National Geographic.

Rivers I., & Duncan N. (2013). *Bullying: experiences and discourses of sexuality and gender.* London : Routledge, Taylor & Francis Group, 2013.

Roland E. (2002). Bullying, depressive symptoms and suicidal thoughts. *Educational Research, 44,* 55-67.

Tittle C. R. (1969). Crime rates and legal sanctions. *Social Problems, 16,* 409-422.

Schenk A. M., & Fremouw W. J. (2012). *Prevalence, psychological impact, and coping of cyberbullying victims among college students.* doi: 10.1080/15388220.2011.630310

Sheldon K. M., & Nichols C. P. (2009). Comparing Democrats and Republicans on intrinsic and extrinsic values. *Journal of Applied Social Psychology 39*(3), 589-623.

Su, Y. (2017). *Dr. Su Statistics.* Retrieved from https://sites.google.com/site/drsustat/

Sylwester K. & Purver M. (2015). *Twitter language use reflects psychological differences between Democrats and Republicans.* doi: 10.1371/journal.

01137422.

U.S. Department of Justice, Office of Justice Programs, Bureau of Justice

Statistics (2010). *Criminal victimization in the United States, 2007*

*statistical tables: National crime victimization survey.* Retrieved from

http://bjs.ojp.usdoj.gov/ content/pub/pdf/cvus0705.pdf

Van Lange, P.A.M., Bekkers, R., Chirumbolo, A., & Leone, L. (2012). Are

conservatives less likely to be prosocial than liberals? From games

to ideology, political preferences and voting. *European Journal of*

*Personality, 26*(5), 461-473.

Vora S. (2014). *The Megan Meier case and its implications.* Retrieved from

http://sites.duke.edu

Zimring, F.E. (1971). Perspectives on deterrence. *NIMH Monograph Series on*

*Crime and Delinquency Issues.* Washington, DC: U.S. Government Printing

Office.

Zimring, F. & Gordon H. (1973). *Deterrence.* Chicago, IL: University of

Chicago Press.

CPSIA information can be obtained
at www.ICGtesting.com
Printed in the USA
LVHW070529261122
733899LV00008B/217